inner yoga

25 Simple Self-Care Tools
for Creative People

inner yoga

25 Simple Self-Care Tools
for Creative People

By Laurie Lamson

JaZzyMaE Media
Oceanside, CA

INNER YOGA
25 Simple Self-Care Tools for Creative People

© 2025 by Laurie Lamson

Photos by Laurie Lamson
Published by JaZzyMaE Media

Email: laurie@creativefreedomnow.com
Publisher site: jazzymaemedia.com
More resources: creativefreedomnow.com

ISBN # 979-8-9997047-3-3

First Edition

TABLE OF CONTENTS

INTRODUCTION

Everyone needs tools to handle overwhelming emotions and life's other challenges, and creative people tend to be more sensitive than the general population.

Unfortunately, when we're suffering, it can be like we have amnesia about how to help ourselves, or there's a strange inner resistance to feeling good.

Sometimes we get caught in a whirlpool of worry and anxiety, and don't know how to climb out of it. And sometimes, we just want to wallow in feeling sorry for ourselves. That's okay. Give yourself permission; there's no need to beat yourself up over it.

The trick is to be able to come out of that mode instead of getting stuck there for long periods of time.

To break through the resistance, or when you're ready to feel better but aren't sure how, these are some effective quick methods. Some may already be known to you.

I encourage you to practice these techniques when you're feeling good so they can become habitual – healthy habits for the mind, body and spirit.

If you make a habit of practicing at least a few, you'll be more likely to remember and reach for them in a crisis.

I recommend keeping this little guide handy, so you have a chance of stumbling across it even if you're feeling bad or stuck in a depressed or amnesia state – to give yourself a better chance of pulling yourself up quickly.

Know that **willingness** is all you need to start on a path of conscious healing, growing, and enjoying life more fully.

Healthy self-care will unfold daily and naturally if you're **willing** to take some responsibility for your own wellbeing and pay attention to your own inner guidance.

You may wish to chronicle your progress. Noticing improvements will increase your intuition, your faith in your own ability to care for yourself, and the feeling of being nurtured and loved.

For the quickest tangible results, use your **imagination.**

Imagination is your bridge between the three-dimensional solid world and the invisible realms of creativity, love, healing life force energy and authentic empowerment. So have fun exercising your glorious imagination!

If your imagination happens to show you anything that scares or upsets you, such as "worst-case scenarios," the techniques in this book can help you resolve and transform that negative energy.

* * *

I've collected, developed, shared and practiced these simple techniques for a long time, and learned firsthand that they really do work.

I sincerely hope and intend that you find them as useful as my clients and I have. If you practice them and allow them to work for you, they will become friends and allies on your journey through life.

- Laurie Lamson

BREATHING

Stopping to take a breath can truly change everything.

When we're stressed, anxious, shocked, or traumatized, we automatically go into the "fight or flight" or "freeze or faint" mode. Our breathing automatically becomes short and shallow.

What is happening on the physical level is that the blood flow to the primitive part of the brain increases, while less blood flows to the front of the brain – the frontal lobe – where we access our genius and creativity.

Taking a few **deep** breaths allows us to reconnect with the frontal lobe. As we calm down, answers and solutions naturally begin to arise in our minds.

Similarly, in the midst of a heated argument, stress and tension mount in our bodies, while our thoughts and feelings quickly turn hostile and defensive. Getting "triggered" into a kneejerk emotional response is not a conscious decision, it just happens.

Stopping to breathe can reconnect us with our conscious thinking ability. It also lets us access feelings of love and forgiveness, helping us to ease out of the fighting mood.

Here are a few very effective breathing techniques you can use any time. They're guaranteed to improve health and wellbeing, especially if practiced on a regular basis.

1. In the Nose, Out the Mouth

Try this while sitting, standing, or lying down.

Breathe in through the nose as deeply as you can. Purse your lips and let your breath out through the mouth.

For a count of four, breathe deeply in through the nose.

For a count of eight, let your breath out through the mouth.

Repeat for one or two minutes, until you feel calmer.

2. Polarity Balance Breath

Stand and cross your arms in front of your chest, hooking your left hand over the right shoulder and right hand over the left shoulder.

Breathe deeply in through the nose and let it slowly out through the mouth.

Re-cross your arms to switch sides and again breath in through the nose and out through the mouth.

Repeat back and forth several times.

3. Somato Respiratory Integration (S.R.I.) for Beginners

Lie down comfortably, close your eyes, and take a deep breath in the nose (for a slow count of four or eight.)

Let it slowly out the mouth.

Repeat for a minute or two, until you feel calm and relaxed.

Now place both hands over your heart and breathe slowly in through the nose, focusing on breathing into the heart. Let it out the mouth.

Place both hands on your belly and breathe in the nose, focusing your breath into your belly. Let it out the mouth.

Bring your hands back to your heart and repeat.

4. B.E.S.T. Breath for Beginners, aka Box Breathing Technique

Breathe in through the nose for a count of four.

Hold it for a count of four.

Breathe out for a count of four.

Rest for a count of four.

Repeat the cycle for at least one to two minutes.

5. B.E.S.T. Breath for Beginners – Deeper Level

This is great to try when dealing with extra stress or panic.

Take a huge deep bellyful of breath and hold it, drop your head and clamp down, tightening up your whole body for a slow count of eight, or longer if you can.

When you finally let the air blow out the mouth, you will most likely experience a big drop in stress, perhaps with a physical shudder or shake as the body releases tension.

(Bio-Energetic Synchronization Technique, or B.E.S.T. program, developed by Dr. M.T. Morter, Jr.)

6. A Balancing Yogic Breathing Technique

Hold your left nostril closed by pushing it down with your left thumb.

Breathe in through the right nostril for a count of four.

Close the right nostril with your left forefinger so both nostrils are now closed.

Take your thumb off the left nostril and let the air out for a count of four or eight.

Breathe in through the left nostril for a count of four.

Close the left nostril with your thumb so both nostrils are closed.

Take your forefinger off your right nostril and breathe out for a count of four or eight.

Repeat going back and forth between the left and right nostrils, for a total of six or eight breaths on each side.

7. Emotional Detox Breathing Treatment

Read through to learn this process, or record yourself reading the instructions out loud and play it back when you're ready to do it. Remember to use your imagination!

Close your eyes and take a deep breath of pure **green healing energy** in through the nose. Let the air out of your mouth.

Breathe in more green healing energy, allowing it to completely fill your whole body, and permeate every cell.

Take another deep breath of green healing energy. This time, on the out breath, intend to release black smoke.

The black smoke might seem to come from your mouth, hands, feet, heart, head, or all over.

You may visualize, sense or feel the black smoke leaving, or simply use your intention to allow it to be gently moved out as it's replaced by the green healing energy.

Continue breathing in the green healing energy, until you get a sense that the releasing black smoke has subsided.

Know, intend and trust that the black smoke is naturally and easily being neutralized and transmuted into light and creative energy.

Now breathe in bright sparkly pink light. Take another deep breath in, filling up every cell in your body with the bright sparkly pink light.

Smile at all your cells filled with the sparkly pink light.

Now open your eyes.

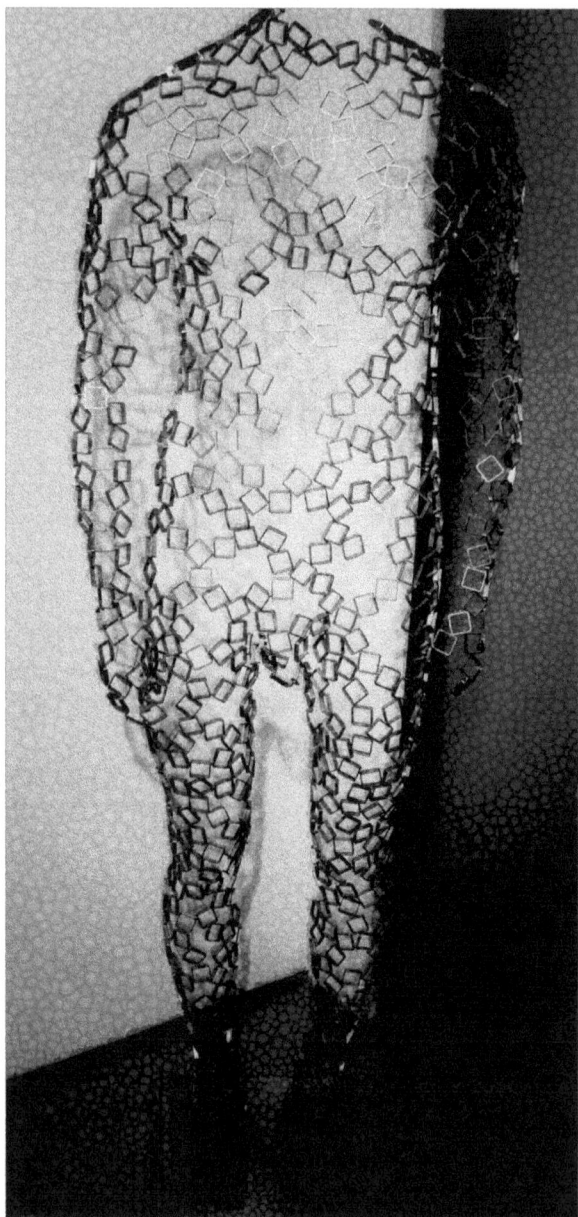

AFFIRMATIONS

Affirmations are statements – sentences we state as facts.

They can be positive statements like, "I can do it," or "I love you."

They can be negative statements, such as, "There's something wrong with you," or "I suck at this."

Affirmations can also be seemingly neutral statements like, "I saw a movie last night," or "I went to my parents' house for Christmas."

Neutral-sounding statements often have a positive or negative emotional charge, depending, for instance, on whether you enjoyed the movie, or your parents nagged you during the holiday.

Negative statements are affirmations of what we don't want, or what we most fear.

They tend to make ourselves and others feel bad.

It's been said that worrying and ruminating on negative thoughts is like praying for what you don't want.

"You're driving sucks!" might help the speaker release tension in the moment, but the overall effect is likely to be negative, for both parties, as well as their relationship, especially if repeated too often.

"I would love for you to drive more defensively," is much more likely to inspire someone to pay attention to the road, or even get motivated to improve their driving skills.

There's a tremendous amount of evidence that our habits of thought and speech affect every aspect of our lives, including our relationships with others.

It may seem obvious in this example about driving, yet it's not that simple to change the ingrained, often unconscious habit of affirming what we most fear or dislike.

Please don't be too hard on yourself, or others, for negative thoughts and statements.

Once we understand how useful it is to affirm what we want, rather than what we don't want, we can practice positive affirmations. With practice, it will become a habit.

Gently become more self-aware, by paying a little more attention to your thoughts. You'll notice that negative thoughts make you feel not-so-wonderful, and when you make negative statements, it tends to cause strife with others.

It will quickly become clear that your choice of words makes a huge difference in how you – and others – feel.

Once you have a list of these negative repeated thoughts or statements, look for a positive version to counter the negative thought that was rattling around in your mind.

Don't say, "I feel good," or "You're a great driver," if you don't believe it. That will just feel like a lie and create unrest inside you.

Rather, something like, "I would love for you to be a great driver," is in alignment with what you want, and it's telling the truth. Think about it, if you're complaining or frustrated about someone's driving, doesn't it mean you want them to pay more attention to the road, speed up, change lanes with confidence, or drive less recklessly?

As often as possible, remind yourself that anything is possible. It *is* possible for your partner to become a more attentive driver. It *is* possible to feel good right now. Regardless of your past experience, it is *possible* to be loved and accepted as you are.

Opening your mind to new possibilities is the stepping-stone to new beliefs, expectations, and experiences.

"I would love for you to drive safely," could still be taken as an insult, especially depending on the feeling energy behind it. Yet it is for sure much closer to what you want than, "You're a f-ing lousy driver!"

Did you know that anxiety and excitement involve the same physiological response? The only difference in how we feel when adrenaline is rushing through our bodies is the type of thoughts we're thinking at the same time.

In other words, the same life force energy can be constructive or destructive. By choosing positive thoughts and statements, we can gain power over our energy and more authority in our own lives.

(Louise Hay was a pioneer of working with positive affirmations for healing and wellbeing. She was able to heal her own body of cancer, and helped facilitate physical and emotional healing in thousands of people, largely through the use of positive affirmations.)

8. I Love Myself

When starting out with affirmations, **"I love myself,"** can be the single most powerful of all.

I recommend repeating it a thousand times a day, any time you can remember it, until it becomes an ingrained habit and makes you feel great to chant it silently to yourself.

This practice may give you an uncomfortably corny or mushy feeling that you might resist at first. That's a sign of having a habit of being too tough on yourself.

It doesn't matter what mistakes you've made, or will make, or what someone else told you about yourself, or harmful behavior patterns you might be caught in, or whatever it is that makes you feel shame, or "less than."

Regardless of any of that, you deserve to love and appreciate yourself, simply because you exist.

So please, just try. Allow yourself to become willing, to be vulnerable enough, at least inside your own mind, to say silly sweet things to yourself.

I guarantee that it will help you lighten up and put a smile on your face. Maybe not at first, but eventually. And it will impact your life experience for the better. I promise.

More affirmations that are helpful to repeat all the time, until they become deeply ingrained beliefs:

I love myself, I love myself, I really, really love myself.

I love myself unconditionally.

I love and accept myself as I am.

All of me approves of me now.

Every day in every way, my life is getting better and better.

I expect to see the best in myself and others.

All I need is within me now.

9. Morning Stretch and Affirmations

Stand facing a window. With a big inhale, stretch your arms above your head, lift up your chin, and say out loud:

I receive my Divine blessings.

Stretch your arms out to the side, and say:

I am open to receiving all good.

Exhale completely as you bend at the waist, drop your arms, reach down to the floor, and say:

I share my gifts with the world.

Roll up, one vertebra at a time, raise your arms above your head with a big inhale, and begin again:

I receive my Divine blessings.

Repeat the cycle three times.

(Adapted from Edgar Cayce and Louise Hay.)

10. a) Instant Feel-Better Affirmation

Try alone or in combination with **#4. B.E.S.T. Breath for Beginners** technique and/or smiling at yourself in the mirror:

Say silently or aloud, twenty times in a row, and mean it:

I want to feel good!

10. b) Get Connected Affirmation

Say silently or aloud, twenty times in a row, and mean it:

I want to connect with my Higher Self.

Feel free to substitute *Higher Self* with *Higher Power, Source Energy, Divine Essence, Divine Intelligence,* or whatever feels the most right and comforting.

(Both adapted from Abraham Hicks and Louise Hay - Louise was also a big advocate of mirror work.)

11. a) Self-Boosting Technique

Imagine standing under a shower of gold light. It streams in through the crown of your head and fills you up and flows down all around your body.

Say silently to yourself, or look in the mirror and say out loud:

There is so much greatness in me
There is so much greatness in me
There is so much greatness in me

There is so much power in me
There is so much power in me
There is so much power in me

There is so much wisdom in me
There is so much wisdom in me
There is so much wisdom in me

There is so much joy in me
There is so much joy in me
There is so much joy in me

There is so much love in me
There is so much love in me
There is so much love in me

I LOVE MYSELF!

(Both 11. a) and b) from author, musician, new-thought teacher Michele Blood.)

11. b) Relationship-Boosting Technique

With eyes closed, imagine someone you'll be meeting, or with whom you want more harmony or a better relationship, standing twelve feet in front of you, standing under the shower of gold light streaming down and filling them up. Silently and sincerely, say to them:

There is so much greatness in you
There is so much greatness in you
There is so much greatness in you

There is so much power in you
There is so much power in you
There is so much power in you

There is so much wisdom in you
There is so much wisdom in you
There is so much wisdom in you

There is so much love in you
There is so much love in you
There is so much love in you

I LOVE YOU!

12. a) Ho'oponopono Mantra

Repeat this silently or aloud to yourself, in any order.

You can also repeat it silently to anyone with whom you have a conflict.

I'm sorry.

Please forgive me.

I love you.

Thank you.

(Hawaiian healing mantra)

12. b) Personalized Ho'oponopono Mantra

Focus on a painful emotion, a part of yourself that feels physically hurt, or intend to connect with your inner child.

Close your eyes and repeat this mantra quietly, personalizing it to the situation, and going with the flow of inspiration.

For example:

I'm so sorry I haven't taken better care of you. Please forgive me for not listening to you. I really do love you. Thank you.

Or:

I'm sorry I was in this accident. Please forgive me for not being more careful. I love you. Thank you.

After a minute or two of consciously repeating this over and over, from the heart, ask that part of you what it wants to tell you.

Listen quietly and let it have its say. Even if what you pick up seems harsh or scary, be like a caring parent listening to an angry or hurt child to gain an understanding of the problem.

Respond with honesty and compassion. Don't make promises you don't know if you can keep, just be open to a dialogue.

When you're ready, ask – your broken heart, your artist self, your wounded inner child, or whatever part of you is in physical or emotional pain – what it wants to tell you.

One of the greatest gifts you can ever give yourself is to become curious about what's going on inside you, and be open to learning *about* yourself, *from* yourself.

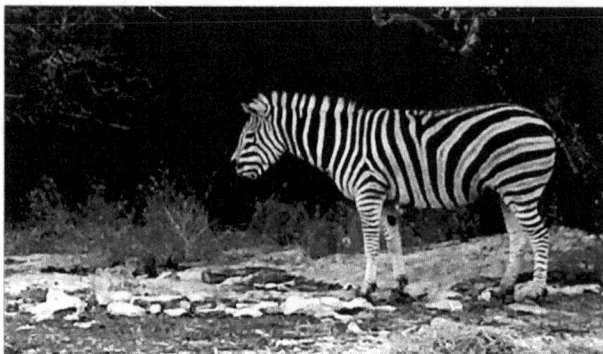

13. a) Hindu Approach to Affirmations

Try chanting an affirmation 108 times in a row, out loud, or silently if you're in public.

You can make it into a chant or a song as you play around with this technique, and perhaps add a rhythm or melody.

For example:

My individuality is safe.

I feel valued and loved.

I'm full of creative energy.

I live and work in harmony with my Higher Self.

I earn a great living doing what I love.

Wonderful things happen through my art.

My work has a powerful positive impact in the world.

13 b) Hindu Approach During Exercise

This is one I use all the time. It helps you enjoy and get the most out of a workout.

While exercising on a Stairmaster, treadmill, elliptical or rowing machine, silently repeat affirmations 108 times, especially those relevant to your goals for your body and health.

For example:

I love my body and my body loves me.

With every step my body forgives and releases the past.

With every breath my body becomes more vibrant.

My body releases excess weight with comfort and joy.

My body is happy, healthy, and fit at every age.

My body accepts and receives everything it needs.

14. Challenge Negative Thought Patterns

We all have ingrained negative thoughts and beliefs we take for granted as accurate or "true," often without testing them or even being consciously aware of them. However, there is a difference between knowledge and belief.

WHAT IF, when you feel bad, it's a sign you're thinking something that's not based on true knowledge; it's just an ingrained, unconscious belief?

WHAT IF, sometimes, in a misguided attempt to protect you, your mind lies to you?

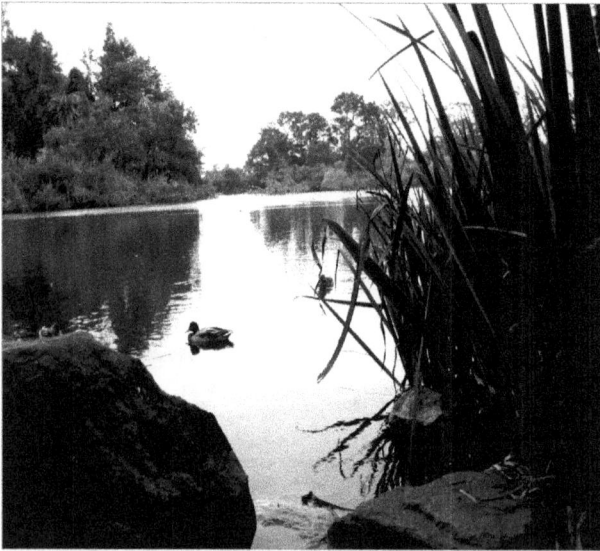

Even if it looks like reality, based on the evidence you see in the three-dimensional world, there's always a broader perspective, and most likely, you're not seeing the whole picture.

Imagine your favorite crackers are missing. You're so used to them being in a particular spot, you literally can't see them, even if they're on the same shelf a few inches away.

(I sure felt silly for insisting someone finished the crackers, when they were right in front of me.)

Our perception is like that; we have blinders blocking our view of whatever we're not expecting.

If we don't expect to be loved, we literally can't feel the unconditional love that's always energetically available.

If we expect our careers to be a struggle and a battle, or believe our goals are impossible for us to achieve, we won't be able to recognize synchronicities, we can't experience doors opening, and we're suspicious of any opportunity. We may self-sabotage, or just give up too easily.

I've personally seen more than one individual with a grouchy, cynical, bitter, or fearful demeanor block assistance that was beyond what they were expecting. With blinders blocking the ability to recognize the help being offered, they shut the door on any assistance, or actively drove help away.

I've also witnessed how an inner attitude of openness and willingness to stretch has a way of opening outer doors to tangible support.

Dr. Mario Martinez, a clinical psychologist specializing in psycho-neuro-immunology, says that if deep down you don't believe you're worthy of the good in life, success and joyful experiences can make you physically ill.

So, if you find yourself believing anything that makes you feel bad, start challenging your own mind on its beliefs. There may be another perspective that you haven't been open to... yet.

For example, many of us deep down unconsciously accept as true: "I'm just not good enough," or, "No one will ever love me," or, all too commonly, "There must be something fundamentally wrong with me."

These may seem like facts, based on your life experience, or your family's and/or society's beliefs and prejudices.

As true as they may seem, they're actually just **beliefs** that you – probably unconsciously – accepted as **facts**.

Now you can begin changing your beliefs.

- Consider that this is most likely a negative belief you accepted and agreed to, rather than an objective fact. This alone will start to bring relief as your mind begins to expand to include new possibilities.

- Try **#12b** to customize the **Ho'oponopono mantra:** acknowledge, and apologize to yourself for the harm this negative belief has done to you.

- Try **#24 Empowering Forgiveness Process** to forgive yourself and others for these limiting, negative beliefs.

- Come up with an affirmation to counter and replace the negative belief, and say it silently and aloud as often as possible.

For example:

I'm good, I'm very good, I'm good enough, I'm enough.

I give and receive with grace and ease.

I accept, approve of, and value myself and my creativity.

All of me is worthy of achieving my goals.

I am a success! I've already accomplished wonderful things.

I earn a lavish, steady, secure income, consistent with integrity and mutual benefits.

My best years are ahead of me.

15. Affirmations as Questions

Negative thoughts and beliefs tend to be a go-to for our minds, such as, "What if (the worst thing happens)?"

One way around this is to create new pathways in the mind, by posing more positive questions.

For example:

What if I'm safe, secure, and protected by unconditional love in every situation?

What if I'm already enough as I am?

How am I becoming healthier, wealthier and wiser?

Why is my art having such a positive impact in the world?

What if I'm an expert at (_____)?

(Adapted from energy healer, Nidhu B. Kapoor.)

16. Prayer to Align with Your Higher Self

Identity is something with multiple moving parts.

We may not always recognize how much choice we have in how we value, prioritize and select what we identify with the most. For example, is it gender, race, sexual preference, religion, nationality, family role, career?

For more inner peace and harmony, stretch your sense of identity and selfhood to a broader perspective – one that includes your Real Self, your Higher Self, your Best Self.

From that broader viewpoint, we can recall that part of our identity is being a member of the human race, the human family. From that perspective, all other people are our brothers and sisters. And that can stretch to include all living things.

The sleeping prophet, Edgar Cayce, said that if you only have one prayer, let it be this:

Please make me a channel of Divine blessings for the highest possible benefit to myself and others.

I added a piece for myself, and I've met others who do the same:

Please make me a channel of Divine blessings for the highest possible benefit to myself, others, and the world in which we live.

MORE ACTIVITIES

Here are some more of my favorite tools and techniques that can help you quickly gain relief in times of trouble. They can shift your perspective and enhance your experience in a variety of ways.

17. Easy African Energy Healing Technique

Count out loud from zero to five, starting quietly and raising your volume with each number (0-1-2-3-4-5.)

Count out loud down from five to zero, lowering the volume with each number (5-4-3-2-1-0.)

Try this several times. (It's a great way to relax and distract yourself while sitting in traffic.)

This is also a fun and harmonizing activity to do in a group. Going around a circle, each person says the next number in the sequence, raising or lowering their volume, depending whether they're going up toward five or down to zero.

(From healer, author and teacher, Ishmael Tetteh.)

18. Release Negative Feelings and Overwhelm

When dominated by heavy sadness, wound-up, nervous anxiety, frustration or rage, physical feelings are a big part of what you're experiencing, so try releasing it physically.

Shake out your arms and legs – it helps your nervous system release and often provides instant relief.

For sadness try running or walking – see **#20. Love Walk.**

For anger and frustration, there's always the old standby, punching a pillow.

A fantastic physical release for any emotion is screaming at the top of your lungs – while alone, not at someone else!

I recommend screaming alone at least once a month, if not once a week.

Refuse to accept the perspective that someone else is wholly responsible for what you're feeling or experiencing. They may have pushed your button, but it is still your button, and you can learn and grow from it.

Deepak Chopra recommends this perspective:

I'm the interpreter of all that I experience, and I have a choice in how I interpret.

19. Small Ball Exercise

If you're feeling especially down, soothe and comfort yourself by curling up in the fetal position: lie on your side, bend your legs in close and wrap your arms around your legs. Take a few deep breaths. Take your time.

Slowly uncurl your body and stretch. Curl back up and rock back and forth.

Stretch out your legs and open your eyes.

Slowly come to a standing position.

Bend at the waist and then slowly roll up, one vertebra at a time.

Spread out your arms to your sides and gently sway left and right.

Bring your hands to your heart and gently sway.

Drop your arms and stand for a moment, feeling safer and more open.

Acting teacher Arthur Lessac's 'Small Ball' technique, as shared by clairvoyant, healer and educator, Judy Nelson.)

20. Love Walk

Take a five-minute walk with just yourself – no cellphone, no music or podcast to distract you. Every time your foot touches the ground, say silently to yourself,

Love.

Really take a look at everything around you. With your attention focused on any one thing – a tree, a flower, a leaf, a crack in the sidewalk, say silently,

Love.

Are you starting to see things differently?

(From healer, life coach, and author, Emmanuel Dagher.)

21. Creativity as Play

Do something that is <u>not</u> your main area of expertise, something you're not "supposed" to be good at. Be like a child and do or make something without being neat or clean, or concerned about results or product – just for the fun of it.

Doodle, fingerpaint, draw an imaginary animal, make a collage (not a vision board,) make up a silly Haiku or song, create a poem or nonsensical statement out of refrigerator magnets, join a drum circle or take a dance class, whatever strikes your fancy!

Playing in other fields just for the joy of it, purely as a process, can refresh your mind and reconnect you with your own creativity. It also reminds you what it feels like to be present and in the flow, without focusing on the past or future.

Let go and have fun. Then, when you're up for it, see if you can bring that relaxed creative attitude to the main task at hand. It may happen anyway, without you even thinking about it.

22. Instead of Resisting, Allow

When we see signs of change on the horizon, or life circumstances simply aren't going our way, the tendency is to resist. Start worrying. Tighten up. Clamp down. Try to control someone else. Try to control what we have no control over.

We resist the unknown. Consciously or unconsciously, we tend to choose, 'The hell I know over the heaven I don't know.'

It's only natural to resist what we don't like and find unacceptable. We resist what hurts or makes us angry: loss of a job, loss of a home, breakup of a marriage, death of a loved one, being bullied, injustice, inequity, gruesome crime, nations at war, a global pandemic.

The problem with resistance is, it does nothing to alleviate our pain and suffering. Instead, it locks us into a battle that we can't win. Especially when what we're resisting has already taken place.

As unpleasant and nerve-wracking as some situations are, the only way to break through to positive solutions is to first allow that which is, or has already occurred.

Seems counterintuitive, *How can I ever allow* that?

Yes, we will have our kneejerk responses, and they may be totally righteous. We also have a choice in how to look at any situation going forward. When you get down to the nubs, there really are only two choices: *resistance* or *allowing*.

Resistance is the path of pain and suffering, remaining stuck, possibly to repeat the same again.

Allowing is the path to change, solutions, synchronicity, growth, freedom, and ultimately, joy. Getting in the habit of allowing will also help you to create more freely.

Here are some tools to resist less and allow more:

1. Acknowledge that change is inevitable. It's a fundamental aspect of being alive, for a snail, a puppy, an ocean wave, a human being. Resisting this fact of life is the cause of a great deal of unnecessary suffering.

2. Trade the *"Why?"* and *"Why me?"* for more potent, useful questions, and <u>don't answer them yourself</u>. Instead, allow answers to arise in your awareness, as gifts from your Higher Self.

What positive lesson can I learn from this?

What is the best that can come from this situation?

What if this is for my highest good?

3. Request a response from the universe:

Please show me all the blessings that can come from this situation.

4. After you acknowledge and start to accept that you can't go backwards, think of what you would like to experience next.

Imagine you're in a little boat, rowing upstream against a current.

Take a deep breath. As you let it out, imagine you're letting go of the oars and drop them in the water.

The current gently turns the boat around and easily maneuvers you downstream.

You are now being guided to a better experience of life. Rejoice!

The **Empowering Forgiveness Process** (#24) will also help increase your ability to be present and in the flow, allowing all of life's blessings.

23. Practice Being Your Own "Doctor"

With a few minutes to spare, make a decision to give an issue or challenge your attention. Have some drinking water on hand and get comfortable, either sitting or lying down.

Address the emotion, pattern, issue, physical symptom or dis-ease directly by speaking to it:

I feel you… I see you… I hear you… I love you.

(You may have trouble saying, *"I love you"* to discomfort and pain at first. Keep going.)

I accept and receive all the positive lessons you have to offer me.

Take a deep breath, let it out, and repeat:

You can heal now. You can heal now. You can heal now. You can heal now. You can heal now.

Take another deep breath, let it out, and say:

You can leave now. You can leave now. You can leave now. You can leave now. You can leave now.

Imagine the issue draining out of your body, down to the center of the earth or maybe being vacuumed away.

It's fine if you don't see anything, just intend that the issue is leaving now.

Have a drink of water.

Trust the process is working, even if the results are not immediate.

(Combines techniques learned from You Wealth Revolution founder, Darius Barazandeh, and energy healer, Nidhu B. Kapoor.)

24. Empowering Forgiveness Process

Forgiveness can be next to impossible when we feel disappointed, abandoned, betrayed, shamed, or violated.

Unwillingness to forgive keeps our attention – and our energy – stuck in the past, unable to create our future. It's often been said that hanging on to resentment is 'like drinking poison and waiting for the other person to die.'

The Maori healers of New Zealand recommend self-forgiveness as one of the crucial keys to healing of any kind, and I agree.

Start with a mantra from Deepak Chopra:

Forgiveness is for me. Forgiveness sets me free.

For deep forgiveness work, try these steps, in any order, and repeat often. if A. is too difficult at first, start with C.

A. *I forgive (so & so) for doing (such & such) to me.*

B. *I allow (so & so) to forgive <u>me</u> for whatever I may have done to them, that made them do (such & such) to me.*

C. *I forgive myself for allowing (so & so) and (such & such) to affect me and my health.*

The final, most challenging step may take a while with the above three steps before you can come to this one sincerely. When you do get here, it feels wonderful.

D. *I give thanks for this situation and I'm glad it happened, because I learned a valuable life lesson that will serve me now and in the future. I wish everyone involved the best.*

(Based on Marianne Williamson's interpretation of forgiveness process from *A Course in Miracles*.)

25. Commune with Nature and Touch Grass

Stand in front of a tree, a flower, a river, a sunset, a bird, or anything else in Nature, and ask if it has a message for you. Or you can pose a specific question about your life.

Close your eyes with your hands facing the natural being to whom you posed the question.

Breathe and quiet your mind.

Wait patiently for whatever you hear with your 'inner ear,' see with your 'inner eye,' or just allow yourself to intuitively pick up a message, even if you don't quite get it yet.

This practice is a great way to develop your intuition and can bring amazingly valuable insights.

Touching grass, walking barefoot on grass or beach sand, and hugging trees can all provide peace and calm.

ABOUT THE AUTHOR

Laurie Lamson is an award-winning writer dedicated to supporting creativity and positive impact.

After extensive training to understand and manage her own energy, she pioneered Soul Medicine and Soulful Space Clearing by combining effective healing techniques for people and places.

Inner Yoga workshops offer an intro to her down-to-earth energy work, and the opportunity to practice these self-care techniques and enjoy guided meditation.

She also offers a **Creative Freedom** group series and a custom one-on-one program designed to empower you on the creative life path in a productive, joyful and abundant way.

Other Books by Laurie

NONFICTION

- *2026 Datebook/Planner for Artists, Writers, Creatives*
- *Now Write! Screenwriting* (anthology – co-Editor)
- *Now Write! Mysteries* (anthology – co-Editor)
- *Now Write! Science Fiction, Fantasy, and Horror* (anthology – Editor)
- *Now Act! Insight, Advice, and Preparation Processes* (anthology – Editor)

FICTION

- *The Second Big Bang* (sci-fi/fantasy novella with a racy sense of humor ;)

MORE RESOURCES

CreativeFreedomNow.com
CreativeFreedom.Shop

YOUR OWN NOTES & AFFIRMATIONS

www.ingramcontent.com/pod-product-compliance
Lightning Source LLC
Chambersburg PA
CBHW071742020426
42331CB00008B/2138